Michael

The Big Red Truck

Elspeth Campbell Murphy
Illustrated by Anne Kennedy

3711

Chariot Books ™
David C. Cook Publishing Co

Chariot Books™ is an imprint of David C. Cook Publishing Co.
David C. Cook Publishing Co., Elgin, Illinois 60120
David C. Cook Publishing Co., Weston, Ontario

THE BIG RED TRUCK
©1990 by Elspeth Campbell Murphy for text and Anne
Kennedy for illustrations

Book and cover design by Dawn Lauck

First Printing, 1990
Printed in Singapore
94 93 92 91 90 5 4 3 2 1

ISBN 1-55513-559-5
LC 88-62946

Michael and his mother went to
the toy store to buy a new truck.
Michael just *loved* trucks!

Michael picked out his
favorite—a shiny red fire engine
with black rubber wheels and a
ladder that really worked.

Michael said, "But this truck is
not for me, right?"

"That's right," said his mother. "You already have one exactly like it at home. This truck is for a little boy somewhere who likes trucks as much as you do, but his mother doesn't have enough money to buy him one. So we will help. God is happy when people who have plenty share with people who don't have enough."

"Now are we going to the little boy's house?" asked Michael.

"No," said his mother. "We don't even know where he lives. We'll take the truck to a special place where people are collecting lots of toys to give to the children at Christmas."

"What special place?" asked
Michael. "Where are we going?"
Mother smiled and whispered a
secret in Michael's ear.
"Wow!" said Michael.

On the way to the special place,
they saw a lot of real trucks.

Michael liked them all very much. But he couldn't wait to see his favorite kind of truck. He knew it would be at the special place, at the—

fire station!

The fire fighters were collecting toys for needy children, and Michael helped. He gave his toy fire engine to a real, live fireman.

The fireman smiled and said, "This will make some little boy *very* happy!"

Then the fireman let Michael
stand on the real fire engine.
"Wow!" said Michael.

All the way home, Michael
thought about driving a fire
engine. But that's not all. He also
thought about how happy God was
that he had shared with another
boy—

a boy like Michael—who just *loved* trucks.

Have you read these books about Michael?

The Big Surprise
Go Home, Squirrel
The Friendly Bear
The Big Red Truck

Look for all the Michael books at your local Christian bookstore.